Contents

Sign and Say

(Book 2)

by

B. M. SUTCLIFFE, BA

Since the publication of SIGN AND SAY, Book 1, in 1981, there has been a marked increase in Sign Language usage on the part of the general public and, consequently, in the number of applicants for RNID Crash Communication Courses. It has become clear that British Signs are used mainly in three ways. It may be best to use the term **'British Sign Usage along a Continuum'** to describe the state of manual communication in the UK at the present time. The essence of this continuum was hypothesised by James Woodward, an American linguist, as having the native, idiomatic Sign Language at one pole and Signed English at the other. Between these two poles the language varieties merge and a range of 'Pidgin' signing occurs.

Signing courses, as provided in the UK, can be identified at three main points along the continuum. These are:

BRITISH SIGN LANGUAGE

Commonly known as BSL, this is taught without spoken English. BSL is not 'sign-word' matched. It is 'sign-concept' based. It does not use English words on the lips with English syntax. It has its own grammar and is a language in its own right. The student is made to think visually with sign concepts and to abandon English, and learn the completely different grammatical structure of BSL.

BRITISH SIGNS SUPPORTING ENGLISH

This is a typical Englishman's compromise and represents a 'give and take' of the two extreme poles of the continuum. Communication is by voiced or unvoiced words (for lipreading) used with English syntax, but the use of such English is carefully monitored. Paraphrasing and simplifying may be used, circumlocation and abstractions avoided, according to the command of English of the communicators. Signs from BSL are matched to the key words of the communication and some of the grammatical features of BSL are employed.

SIGNED ENGLISH

Currently being developed, this system matches traditional British Signs to specific English words and uses English syntax. Where traditional signs are insufficient or inadequate, newly-generated signs are formed but these have to be agreed as 'acceptable' by the adult deaf persons serving on the Signed English Working Party. There are, in addition, generated signs for the grammatical inflexions of English.

A British version of the Signing Continuum might then look like this:

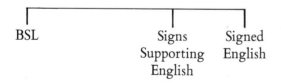

Of the three main methods of British Sign Usage it might be said that BSL is a valued everyday method of communication amongst born-deaf people themselves.

(An excellent laymen's guide to this usage can be found in *British Sign Language* by Margaret Deuchar, published by Routledge and Kegan Paul.) 'British Signs Supporting English' is commonly used when deaf people like to use lipreading as well as signing and when the communicators may be mixed hearing and deaf. 'Signed English' is an educational tool for use in the classroom.

The term **'Total Communication'** is one which is in use nowadays. It was originally conceived as a philosophy which would incorporate any combination of known and recognised methods of communicating with deaf people. The theory of this was widely accepted after its proposal by David Denton, Maryland School for the Deaf, USA, in 1970. But, in practice, it has had such loose application that it has come into some disrepute because of the implication that 'Total Communication' means anything that the communicator wishes it to mean. To many deaf people it does seem to mean 'please speak clearly and sign at the same time'. This, again, is a compromise situation, much in line with Signs Supporting English. The receiver of a signed/spoken communication, who has a reasonable command of English, does not require every single little function word to be signed, nor does he/she require grammatical information such as the verbal inflexions for 'swim', 'swims', 'swimming', 'swam', 'have swum'. The basic sign 'swim' is sufficient as the context of the word, her/his general knowledge of

English grammar, and the clear lipspeaking pattern, will ensure reception of a normal English sentence. When command of English is limited this communication may well have to be paraphrased or simplified. If the command of English is very minimal then the preferred mode of communication is very likely to be BSL.

Whichever of the three main usages is adopted it is a source of some gratification that *all* take their core vocabulary from traditional British Signs.

SIGN AND SAY, Book 1, was a best-seller from the moment of its publication. It is hoped that in offering a further 337 signs, this Book 2 will be helpful to those seeking to use British Signs in whatever chosen method of application.

REFERENCES

Denton, D.M. 'The philosophy of Total Communication. *British Deaf News,* supplement, August 1976.

Deuchar, M. *British Sign Language.* Routledge & Kegan Paul, 1984.

Woodard, J.C. Jnr. 'Implicational lects on the deaf diglossic continuum. Unpublished PhD dissertation, Georgetown University 1973.

Due to the difficulty of putting three-dimensional signs on to a flat, printed surface, misunderstandings may occur in the execution of certain signs. In addition, the user must be aware of the importance and use of facial expression in signing which is not easy to portray on a static photograph.

Regional variations in signing must also be considered. The learner must check that the signs which are demonstrated are appropriate for use in his/her own area.

The SIGN AND SAY books are only designed to act as primers. Contact with deaf people is essential for real learning to take place.

ABOUT (meaning approximately)
Move spread hand round horizontally
in circles.

ACCOUNTS
Flick all fingers whilst moving hands upwards
(as if skimming up two columns of figures).

ACCUSE
Point index fingers forward with two or
three jabs.

ACTOR — Take closed hands in and out from
chest alternately. Make a slight strutting motion
with the body.

ADDRESS — Hold left hand still with fingers
together. Take spread fingers of right hand
straight across outside of left hand.

ADMINISTRATION
Move hands alternately in and out from chest
as though controlling reins.

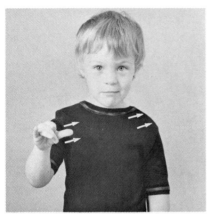

AEROPLANE — Extend thumb and little finger whilst keeping three middle fingers bent. Make an ascending movement across chest.

AFTER — Left hand represents a 'time' hand. Roll right fist with extended thumb from body, forwards over wrist of left hand.

AGAINST (or 'Object to')
Keep left hand still. Push right fist (with extended little finger) away from body.

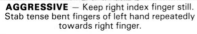

AGGRESSIVE — Keep right index finger still. Stab tense bent fingers of left hand repeatedly towards right finger.

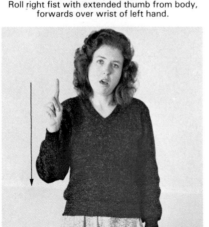

ALONE
Take single out-turned finger straight down.

ALONG — Make small circular movements with index finger moving outwards from body whilst doing so.

AMONG — Left hand makes small circles. Right hand makes larger circles over it. Both circles are horizontal and outwards from body.

ANSWER
Stroke ball of left thumb twice briskly with tip of right index finger.

ANYWAY
Make alternate bouncing movements up and down with each hand.

ANALYSE (or Research)
Bring both lots of knuckles together and out sideways again two or three times (as if teasing out something).

APPRENTICE
Right hand grip takes left hand gently forward.

ARCHITECT
With two extended fingers draw a straight line down edge of arm and hand.

ARGUE
Make alternate up and down movements of friction with two crooked fingers.

ART
Keeping the two fingers together make quick etching movements as if touching up a painting.

AUTOMATIC
Make very quick little circles round and round the same spot, jabbing outwards each time.

ATTENTION
Bring flat vertical hands straight down in parallel.

ATTRACT
Hands lightly touch clothes as body moves sideways.

ASSOCIATION — Clasp hands upside down on one another and move slowly round in horizontal circle away from body.

AUTUMN
Wiggle fingers diagonally downwards to represent leaves falling.

AVERAGE — Keep slightly spread left hand still. Skim the blade of upright right hand to and fro over tips of left fingers.

AVOID
Push out turned hand away from shoulder. Turn head away to left whilst doing so.

BACON
Move the two thumbs and fingers apart making slight wiggly movements whilst doing so.

BADMINTON
Jerk wrist forward with a quick flicking movement.

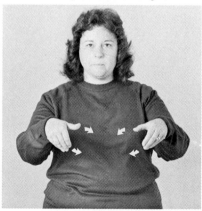

BAKER
With repeated movement imitate mixing dough.

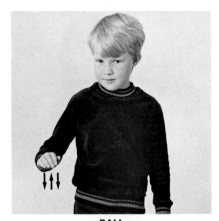

BALL
Bounce hand down and up.

BANANA
Imitate holding banana in left hand and peeling it with right pinched thumb and finger.

BATTERY
Move pinched thumb and index finger from lower lip down chin.

BEFORE (meaning 'in the past')
Take angled hand back over shoulder.

BEGIN — Hold left hand still. Jerk right hand thumb upwards high on chest then sharply drop whole of right hand down behind left hand.

BET
Keep left hand still. Slap the back of right hand down on to left palm.

BELIEVE (Part 1) — Move index finger straight down from forehead towards open left palm. Change right hand into vertical open hand.

BELIEVE (Part 2)
Bring vertical open hand from Part 1 smartly down at right angles on to open left palm.

BETWEEN
Hold left hand still (with middle fingers apart) and rock flat right hand from side to side of 'V'.

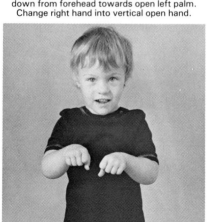

BICYCLE
Rotate fists forward alternately.

BIRO
Hold hand still but flick thumb down and up.

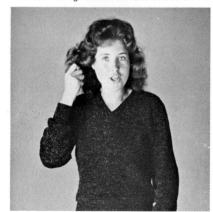

BIRTHDAY (Children's sign)
Tug an imaginary tuft of hair twice.

BLANKET
Grab top of imaginary blanket with each hand and pull well up over chest to chin level.

BOTH (Alternative to sign on p. 25, Book 1)
Bring index and middle finger together.

BREAD
Keep left hand still. Push top hand forwards and backwards to imitate sawing.

BRIDE — With palms inward outline a veil. On reaching shoulder level twist palms outward and make an elegant tapering movement down body and slightly away behind hips.

BRIDESMAID
Imitate holding a posy.

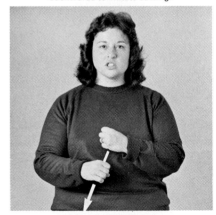

BRUSH (or Sweep)
Keeping fists apart move both hands down and up together.

BURGLAR
Place 'V' fingers at side of eye. Move fingers a short way sideways closing at the same time.

BURN
Strike side of one thumb down side of the other.

BUSY
Hold left hand still. Repeatedly stab blade of right hand on to top edge of left index finger.

BUY — Hold left hand still. Bend fingers of right hand and bring this smartly down to strike against left palm.

CAMEL
Clasp both hands separately and make floppy steps alternately. Jerk wrist outwards each time.

CANADA
Imitate holding coat lapel and shaking off snow.

CARAVAN — Hook right index finger through loop of left thumb and finger. Move both along a straight line across chest.

CATERPILLAR
Move bent index finger along in small humps.

CENTRE — With middle finger pointing down make a horizontal circle then take middle finger straight down to centre of left palm.

CHARACTER
Form right thumb and index finger into a large 'C' and move straight down centre of body.

CHEAP — Keep left hand still. Bring extended two fingers of right hand down towards extended two fingers of left hand.

CHEAT
Take thumb-nail straight down cheek with crafty-looking face.

CHEEKY
Pinch cheek.

CHEMICAL — As if holding a small test tube between each thumb and forefinger move gently up and down alternately.

CHERRIES
Hook fingers down near upper lobe of ear.

CHEW — Make horizontal circular movements with both hands. Top hand makes a slightly bigger circle and follows round after bottom hand.

CHICKEN (or Hen)
Flap both elbows down to touch waist and repeat.

CHIPS — Begin with each thumb and finger slightly apart. Pull each sharply to the side with a pinch. Repeat three or four times.

15

CHRISTIAN
Outline a small cross on forehead with the thumb.

CLASS — Make two 'C' hands. Move them out from body in a circle until outside blades of little fingers meet.

CLOUDS
Make semi-circles towards head (opposite way to freedom of 'space').

COMMON
Keeping flat hands together move both round in a horizontal circle.

COMMUNITY
Keeping hands fixed together move out and round in horizontal circle.

COMPETITION — Bring top index fingers to meet. Repeat this downwards (as if indicating two names of people opposing each other).

CONCORDE
Zoom right index finger down across chest.

CONCEITED (or Snobbish)
Use tip of index finger to tilt nose upwards.

CONCENTRATE
Take pointed fingers down and forward to meet at a focal point.

COMPUTER — Make continuous circles with forefingers each going in opposite direction. (Both go outwards at top and inwards at bottom of circle.)

CONFUSED — Make inward moving circles over forehead with spread clawed hands. Circles should slightly overlap.

CONTINUE
Place two thumb tips together and move hands straight out from body.

CORNER
Bring tips of fingers to meet at a right-angle.

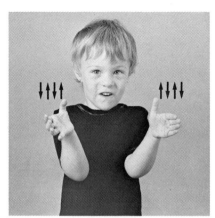

CORNFLAKES
Hold imaginary box of cornflakes and shake up and down.

COUGH
Beat inside of clenched fist on to chest twice.

COWBOY
Imitate firing two guns.

CRAB
Pinch thumb and finger together rapidly and move slightly forward away from body.

CRASH
Hold left hand still. Bring right fist rapidly over to strike left palm.

CRICKET
Imitate short forward stroke with bat.

CRIPPLED (or Spastic)
Lean slightly to one side and stab index fingers
up and down alternately.

CRITICISE
Both fists have extended little finger. Move them
alternately in circular motion away from body.

CROWD — Hunch shoulders, press little fingers
of both fists together and lurch body slightly
from side to side.

CUCUMBER — Keep left looped thumb and
finger still. Use right blade of hand to make
quick repeated chopping movements.

CURTAINS
Hold imaginary edge of curtains
and draw together.

CUSHION (or Sponge)
Bounce both sets of fingers up and down
on thumbs.

DECORATING (Painting)
Angle hand forward and straighten again
alternately, imitating slap-on brushwork.

DECREASE (or Less)
Bring hands downwards and inwards.

DEEP
Circle finger in downward spiral then plunge
finger tip straight down.

DEER
Move hands outwards and upwards for further
branching of antlers.

DEFEAT
Use flat right hand to press down left fist.

DEFEND
Push fists firmly away.

DETECTIVE
Flick thumb forwards to reveal hidden badge behind lapel.

DINNER — Use extended fingers to represent knife and fork and move hands up and down alternately towards mouth.

DIVINE
Point flat hand well above head and bring down in straight line over middle of face.

DOLL
Hold body stiff. Make stiff clockwork movements up and down alternately with each arm.

DOLLAR — Keep left flat hand still. Place right thumb behind left fingers and clasp left hand. Pull right hand away sharply. Repeat.

DOUBLE
Shake both fingers side to side.

DROWN
Keep left hand still. Gradually close fingers of right hand and move it down behind left hand.

DRUNK
Rock the two fingers alternately on and off the left palm with a matching body lurch.

DUCK
Extend index and middle fingers. Make these open and shut on ball of thumb.

DURING — Brush bottom blade of right hand right through 'V' space of thumb and other fingers on left palm.

EACH
Gently stab finger-nail forward to three or four separate points in horizontal line.

EASY
Pinch top of limp little finger of left hand and wiggle it.

EMPLOYER (or Boss)
Strike forefinger forwards authoritatively two or three times.

ENCOURAGE
Make small repeated pushing movements forward with both hands at same time.

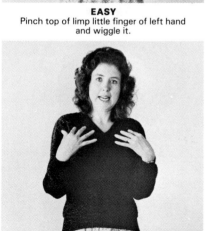

ENEMY (or Attack)
Bring spiked fingers of both spread hands sharply towards upper chest.

ENGAGED — Point to imaginary diamond on ring finger. Slightly agitate right finger tip to represent the sparkle.

ESCAPE
Keep left hand still. Shoot right index finger speedily under left elbow.

23

EVERY
Flick all fingers forward off cheek in a
fan-like movement.

EXPENSIVE
Shake limp open hand up and down
(= 'pain near pocket').

EXPLAIN
Circle flat hands outwards alternately. Dip palms
slightly down as hands go forward.

FALL
Keep left hand still. Suddenly tip the two right
fingers forward and over.

FALSE
Tap end of nose with middle finger.

FAR OFF
Peer into the distance.

FILING — Make angled right hand dip down behind left palm then jump up over left thumb and dip again in front of left hand.

FILM
Keep left hand still. Turn imaginary handle forwards and back in circular motion.

FIND
With thumb and finger almost in 'C' shape lift hand from waist level up to cheek level.

FIREMAN
Raise and lower imaginary fire-hose.

FISH AND CHIPS
Keep thumb still but wiggle fingers repeatedly.

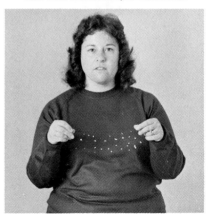

FLOUR
Wiggle fingers with a sprinkling movement.

'FLU
Make two quick plucking movements off nose
and downwards and outwards.

FOG
Frown slightly and peer ahead as open hands
zig-zag at sides of face.

FOOTBALL
Flick underside index finger up sharply to
push away from top finger.

FORK
Stab the two extended fingers towards palm
of left hand.

FORTNIGHT — Keep left hand still with
extended index finger. With two extended
fingers on right hand push it out across left
index finger.

FRIDAY
Keep left fingers still. With right fingers make
small rubbing circles over left fingers.

FULL
Keep left hand still and bring right hand
gradually up to touch it.

FUTURE
Project angled right hand forward
from side of face.

GALLAUDET COLLEGE (in America)
Take thumb and finger away from corner of eye
in a pinched movement.

GIRL
Short single stroke down cheek with inside of
right index finger.

GLORY
Keeping spread hands almost upright bring them
right down to hips with rapid wiggling fingers.

GO
Briskly swing finger out and away from body.

27

GOAL — Make 'V' shape with fingers on one hand and direct straight index finger of other hand towards gap.

GREASY
Rub ball of each thumb across fingers three times with unpleasant expression on face.

GUILTY (my fault)
Strike blade of right little finger against chest twice.

HAMBURGER
Place fingers and thumb around imaginary hamburger and move towards mouth.

HANDICAPPED — Place right bent hand between thumb and fingers of left hand. Draw both back towards body.

HAPPEN
Hold left hand still. Move pointed right index finger up suddenly.

HEALTHY
Briskly stroke flat hand down body twice.
(Keep thumb up.)

HEARING-AID
Make slight screwing movement to push
imaginary small button into ear.

HELICOPTER
Point index finger upwards and circle it several
times horizontally.

HILL
Keeping palm tilted outwards outline of hill away
and over.

HOME (going home)
Take angled hand out and slightly downwards.

HONOUR
Take flat hands down from forehead and gently
incline head forward.

HORSE
Place two separated fingers of right hand astride two side-turned fingers of left hand.

HORSE-RIDING
Keep left fist firmly on top of right fist and move both up and down together.

HOW
Cross fingers as if to fingerspell 'W' but separate fingers again then rejoin the 'W'.

HUMBLE
Lower both hands slowly.

HUNDRED
Sweep finger under full outline of chin. (Two fingers = 200 etc.)

ICE-CREAM
Hold imaginary cone and move hand up and down from nose to chin area.

IDEA
Flick up index finger and move thumb away from forehead.

IF
Twist wrist forwards and backwards so that extended little finger follows the direction.

ILL (seriously)
Stroke little fingers once down body.

IMAGINE
Almost touch right forehead with tip of right index finger then circle it upwards and away.

IMPORTANT
Place centre palm of left hand on tip of right index finger and raise both together.

IMPROVE
Hold left flat hand still. Move blade of right hand steadily up left palm.

INDIGESTION
Angle the right hand in towards chest and rub
finger tips up and down one central spot.

INFLUENCE
Hold left hand still. Bunch right fingers on top
then suddenly release and spread them out.

INSTITUTE
Place right fist firmly on back of left hand then
press both firmly down a short way.

INTERESTING
Move slightly clawed hands alternately up and
down chest area.

INTERPRETING
Swing the two pairs of fingers backwards and
forwards alternately.

INTERRUPT — Make a 'V' gap between
middle and ring fingers then hold left hand still.
Push flat right hand through and back with
several short jerks.

INTRODUCE
Cross palms over to the opposite sides.

JAM — Hold left hand still. Rub underside of right fingers backwards and forwards on left palm with slapping motion.

JELLY
Keeping spread hands stiff shake both keeping in horizontal plane.

JUMPER
Jump both angled hands (with bunched fingers) from upper chest down to waist level.

JUST
Bounce angled hand quickly on and off front of shoulder.

KIND (or Gracious)
Bring thumbs up from heart area and tilt them outwards from body.

33

KITCHEN
Fingerspell 'K' but tap right knuckle twice against left index finger.

KNEEL
Bend first two fingers of right hand and place knuckles down on left palm.

KNIT
Alternate index fingers up and down with a slight brushing off criss-cross movement.

KNOW
Place a thumb tip on forehead.

LADY
Outline edge of a bolero.

LANGUAGE — Make two capital 'L' shapes with thumb and index finger of each hand and draw them slightly apart.

LEAD (or Guide)
Clasp right hand over left fingers then take both hands together across and out from body.

LEAN
Move tilted right flat hand towards fingers of left upright flat hand.

LEND
Cross two 'fist' hands at the wrist and move both outwards from body.

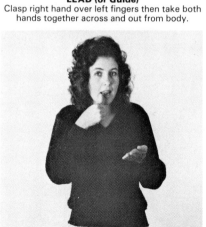

LETTER
Put tip of thumb on tip of tongue and then press ball of right thumb on to left palm.

LIBRARY — Using blade of hand make three or four chopping movements forward moving hand to the right at same time (indicating books).

LION
'Walk' each clawed hand forward alternately.

LIP-READ
Keep index and middle finger extended and move in circle around lips.

MANY
Wiggle all fingers whilst moving hands slightly apart.

MAYBE — With fingers spread rock the hand slightly so that thumb and little finger go up and down alternately.

MARRY (Part 1)
Imitate sliding ring on to 'ring' finger.

MARRY (Part 2)
Finish the movement of Part 1 by placing palm flat down on to left hand.

MAYOR (or President)
With bent fingers move hands down (in slight jumps) towards imaginary central badge.

MEASURE — Pinch thumb and index finger of each hand (as if holding tape-measure) and pull slightly apart.

MEET
Move index fingers towards each other.

MEETING (noun) — Each index finger makes outwards circular movements but hands overlap slightly whilst doing so.

MILK
Imitate action of milking, pulling down on each hand alternately.

MONEY — Rub thumb on fingers of right hand and at the same time repeatedly drop an imaginary coin on to left palm.

MONKEY
Imitate upward scratching movements with curled fingers.

MOON — Make a crescent shape downwards. Begin with thumb and finger pinched, open out a little then taper off again.

MOST
Hold left index finger still. Strike right index finger down and past left finger.

MOUNTAIN
Move flat hands upwards towards central peak but keep well out and above eye-level.

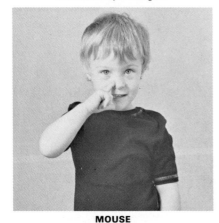

MOUSE
Screw tip of finger round in crease of nose.

MUMMY
Tap three fingers on side of forehead.

MURDER
Stab the three fingers of the letter 'M' into side of throat.

MUSIC
Move both fingertips outwards and inwards
together.

MUST
Bring both open flat hands emphatically
downwards.

MYSELF — Use the sign for 'my' and add 'self'.
Take extended forefinger straight down midline
of body.

NAVY
Swing both hands over to opposite hip.

NEAR
Keep left hand still. Bring right hand near to it.

NEARLY — With thumb-nail tucked into crook
of right index finger shake wrist forward twice.
Narrow the eyes.

NUTS
Knock heel of lower palm twice up to underside of chin.

OF
Use thumb and index finger to make two short parallel curves outwards.

OPERATION
Take tip of thumbnail straight down. (This can be done on any appropriate part of the body.)

ORANGE (Colour or fruit)
Hold clawed hand near side of mouth and squeeze fingers downwards.

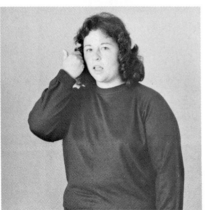

PALE
Stroke outside of hand in one slow movement down cheek.

PARK
Bring arm diagonally up across chest with a sharp movement and hold it.

PARTY — Twist both wrists inwards and outwards quickly so that both little fingers flick in and out together.

PARTY (alternative sign)
Circle both hands round continuously in opposite directions as if waving two flags.

PEOPLE — Touch forehead quickly then bring upright index finger down to one or two points (= counting heads).

PHOTOGRAPHY — Spread hand near front of face. Draw hand away and bunch fingers and thumb at the same time.

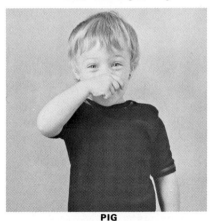

PIG
Rub inside of fist round and round nose.

PILOT
Grip the imaginary bottom arc of a steering wheel and push slightly forward.

PINK
Suddenly burst open thumb and finger to match
explosive sound of 'P' on the lips.

PITY (or Mercy)
Make stroking movements with hand as if
saying 'poor pussy'.

PLATE
Use right index finger to draw a circle over left
palm starting near left thumb.

PLAY
Make circular outward movements with both
hands in horizontal plane.

PLAYING CARDS — Tilt open left hand slightly
towards body. With right hand take imaginary
card and place forward on imaginary table.
Repeat.

PLENTY
Bring upper side of hand up to chin
and brush past it twice.

POINT
Slightly screw right fingertip on to left palm centre.

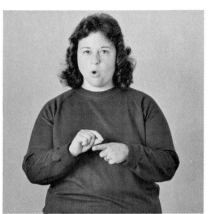

POISON — Hold left extended index finger still. Pinch right thumb and index finger and move along top edge of left finger.

POPE
With two extended fingers make small sign of Cross.

POSH
Stroke side of nose briskly twice with conceited look on face.

POST
Hold left 'gap' hand still. Insert angled right hand into gap.

PRECIOUS
Hug fists towards chest and press together.

PRINCE
Use two extended fingers to outline
a row of medals.

PRINCESS
Use spread hand slightly cupped to indicate
diamond tiara (centrepiece).

PRINT
Press fist rather sharply down and up
on left palm. Repeat.

PROMISE (Part 1) — Move index finger straight
down from mouth towards open left palm.
Change right hand into vertical open hand whilst
doing so.

PROMISE (Part 2)
Bring vertical hand from Part 1 smartly down
at right angles on to left palm.

PROOF
Keep right finger pressed on left palm and push
left palm forwards and outwards.

44

QUARTER
Fingerspell 'Q' but tap left index finger twice into left-hand loop.

RAIN — Bring hands down together whilst flicking the fingers continuously and delicately. Repeat the movement.

REFEREE
Hold imaginary whistle to bottom lip then pull slightly away.

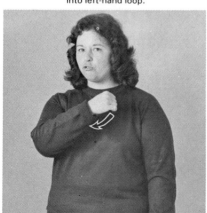

REFUSE
Bring fist sharply out from upper chest turning outwards whilst doing so.

REMIND
Jab fingertips of angled right hand twice rather sharply on front of right shoulder.

REPAIR
Rotate cupped hands backwards and forwards alternately.

RESPONSIBLE
Press hand down slightly on shoulder.

RICE
Wiggle fingers across lower lip.

RIVER
Keep hands parallel and move forwards
in meandering way.

ROMAN
Hold thumb flat on top of head.

ROYAL — Sweep the angled slightly out-turned
hand downwards diagonally (as though outlining
the Queen's blue sash).

RUBBISH — Make rapid circular movements up
and away with right finger. Finish with a straight
toss-away movement.

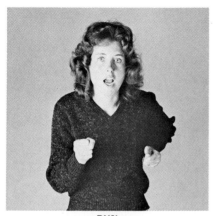

RUN
Move fists alternately forwards and backwards leaning slightly forwards from waist.

RUSSIA
Hold fist still after military flourish.

(THE) SACK
Hold right finger still. Brush left finger off and out once briskly.

SAD — Draw extended index finger straight down middle of face and drop head forward slightly at same time.

SAILING
Fix right hand at right angles to left and move both forward together.

SAILOR
Swing hands round to reverse positions of right hand behind back and left flat hand in front.

47

SALAD
With spread cupped hands mime tossing a salad.

SALT
Rub two fingers backwards and forwards on ball of thumb.

SAND
Rub fingers along ball of thumb and make little sprinkling movements at same time.

SANDWICH
Press two hands together.

SATISFIED
Take slightly angled hand from upper chest to lower chest area.

SATURDAY
Flat hand makes one full circle around back of left hand.

SAY
Take finger-tip straight forward away from mouth.

SCOTLAND — Keep hand still. Use pressure of inside elbow to squeeze imaginary wind-bag of bagpipes in and out.

SCREAM
Release all fingers suddenly whilst pushing hand forward.

SEEMS
Slightly tilt spread hand once or twice as if throwing up reflection from a mirror.

SELL
Turn hands suddenly outwards flicking them upside down whilst doing so.

SERVE — Keeping two stiff fingers on each hand make elegant move forwards and slightly outwards turning fingers upside down.

49

SEW
Keep left hand still. Take right pinched thumb and finger down and up.

SEWING MACHINE
Move hands slowly forward in parallel then repeat.

SEXUAL INTERCOURSE
Lock both open hands together between thumb and fingers.

SHEEP — Make several forward circles with little fingers extended, but do not move hands forward from side of head.

SHOP
Dig spread fingers downwards with firm movement.

SHOULD (or 'ought to') — Twist clenched fist down then in towards body and turned upside down (a short, emphatic movement).

SIMILAR
Slightly raise and lower each extended index
finger alternately.

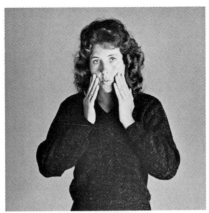

SOAP
Make small circular massage movements
on cheeks.

SON
Two fingers rub side to side under chin
('Boy' is signed with one finger).

SOON
Rub thumb and finger together several times.

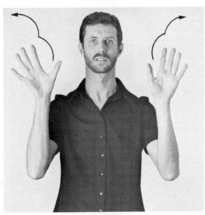

SPACE
Take spread hands up and out in semi-circular
movements.

SPADES (Playing cards) — Dig fingertips
down then half cup hand upwards and outwards
with quick throwing out movement.

SPAIN — Clap fingers down on to palms with a flourish as if using castanets. Raise and lower each arm alternately.

SPECIAL — Take looped thumb and index finger slightly forward with an emphatic movement and hold it.

SPIDER
Wiggle the fingers all the way down.

SPOON
Pinch thumb and index finger and make small circles as if stirring.

STAMP
Take two fingers from lips and press tips down on palm of left hand.

STRAWBERRY
Gently stroke fingers off nose and down to bunched position twice.

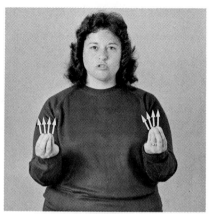

STRIKE
Jerk both hands upwards releasing fingers suddenly.

STRING
Whilst twirling thumb with forefinger of each hand move hands apart.

SUN
Release fingers suddenly and beam the hand slightly towards face.

TALK
With extended index fingers tap one hand on top of another.

TAX
Hold left index finger still. Chop right finger tip down past left one.

TELL
Move sideways-finger straight from mouth (note difference from 'say').

53

TENNIS
Imitate preparing to serve.

THEATRE
Keep left hand still. Slightly wiggle middle finger
of right hand (to imitate a ballerina).

THESE
Spread hand outwards in a fan-like movement
fairly near the waist.

THING — Tip the two index fingertips together
and away several times moving hands along
straight line at same time.

THOSE
Spread hand outwards in a fan-like movement
about a foot away from the waist.

THOUSAND — Bring right thumb across chest
and slightly dig in thumb-nail to a point in left
breast-pocket area.

TOILET
Rub tip of middle finger up and down front of shoulder two or three times.

TOMORROW — Take pointed finger straight forward is semicircular arched movement brushing finger nail against cheek.

TOOTHBRUSH
Move fingertip up and down all the way along teeth.

TYPING
Flick fingers up and down randomly.

UGLY
Make a zig-zag movement down middle of face with inside edge of flat hand.

UNCLE
Move two slightly bent fingers from right side of chin to touch left side.

UNDERSTAND
Keep thumb still on forehead but flick up bent index finger.

UNEMPLOYED — Hold left hand still. Fix right vertical hand on it then sweep off the right hand with emphatic movement.

USE
Stroke side of thumb tip twice down middle of chin.

VALLEY
Tilt palms outwards as flat hands outline a dip.

VERY
Keep left hand still, brush 'V' of right fingers straight off left palm.

VIDEO
Use 'V' fingers and take both hands round a flat circle in same direction at same time.

VISIT
Take two 'V' hands outwards from body
(but this is a directional sign).

WAGES
Pull spread hand down slightly and bunch
fingers and thumb at same time. Repeat.

WAIT
Drop two flat hands slightly but with an
emphatic movement.

WAKE UP (Part 1)

WAKE UP (Part 2)
Suddenly release thumb and finger,
open eyes and lift up face brightly.

WALES
Curl three fingers forward (representing three
feathers of Prince of Wales insignia).

WALK
Move each finger forward alternately in small
'steps' on palm of left hand.

WASHING
Rub top knuckles backwards and forwards over
bottom clasped hand.

WEATHER
Waft hand forwards towards face slightly
bunching fingers each time.

WET
Rub thumbs across tips of all fingers repeatedly.

WHICH
Move right forearm several times left and right
keeping thumb and little finger extended.

WHISPER

WINDOW
Hold left hand still. Move right flat hand up and down to represent sash window movement.

WINE — Little finger and thumb remain touching. The other three fingers make repeated small circles forward and back to cheek.

WOOD
Make two chopping movements with blade of right hand into 'V' gap of left hand.

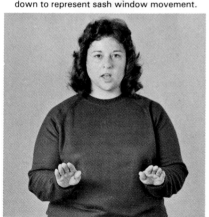

WITHOUT (Part 1)
Draw downturned palms towards body turning them upside down in process.

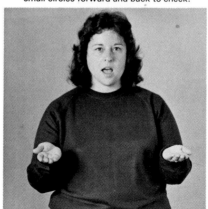

WITHOUT (Part 2)
Finish by displaying hands in palm upward position.

WON'T — Begin with fingers fully clasped by cheek. Push hand out and away from face releasing fingers and turning outwards at same time.

WOOL — Pull back right thumb and fingers sharply till they bunch together. Make this plucking movement up left arm.

WORLD
Outline a globe.

YELLOW
Flick index finger up from ball of thumb twice, near lobe of ear.

YESTERDAY
Move pointed finger backwards behind ear in semicircular arched movement.

YOUNG
Brush back of hand upwards on cheek twice with a lively look on face.

ZIP — Right pinched thumb and finger touches left pinched thumb and finger and then zips up. (Keep left hand still.)

CAN'T BE BOTHERED
Make loose 'C' shaped hand and flop it forwards and downwards.

HAVEN'T GOT
Move slightly cupped hand sharply across mouth with tossing out movement.

HAVING AN AFFAIR — Clasp fingers of both hands and hold still. Wiggle thumbs alternately up and down but hidden behind fingers.

HOW MUCH?
Move tips of fingers out and away from chin with questioning look on face.

HOW OLD
Wiggle fingers down from nose area.

MIND YOUR OWN BUSINESS
Move two extended fingers down and away from nose briskly.

INDEX TO PICTURES

	Book	Page No.		Book	Page No.		Book	Page No.
BETTER	1	21	BREAD	2	12	CAREFUL	1	28
BETWEEN	2	11	BRIDE	2	12	CARELESS	1	29
BICYCLE	2	11	BRIDESMAID	2	12	CARPENTER	1	29
BIG (see 'LARGE')	1	55	BRING (or FETCH)	1	26	CASTLE	1	29
BIRD	1	22	BROTHER	1	26	CAT	1	29
BIRO	2	11	BROWN	1	26	CATERPILLAR	2	14
BIRTHDAY	2	11	BROWNIE (see 'GIRL GUIDE')	1	49	CENTRE	2	14
BISCUIT	1	22	BRUSH (or SWEEP)	2	12	CERTAIN (see 'SURE')	1	76
BISCUIT (Alternative)	1	22	BUILD	1	26	CHAIN	1	29
BITTER	1	22	BURGLAR	2	13	CHAIR	1	29
BLACK	1	22	BURN	2	13	CHAPLAIN (see 'CLERGYMAN')	1	31
BLANKET	2	12	BUS	1	27	CHARACTER	2	14
BLIND	1	23	BUSY	2	13	CHEAP	2	14
BLOOD	1	23	BUT	1	27	CHEAT	2	14
BLUE	1	23	BUTTER	1	27	CHEEKY	2	15
BLUE (Alternative)	1	23	BUTTERFLY	1	27	CHEESE	1	30
BLUSH	1	22	BUY	2	13	CHEMICAL	2	15
BOAT	1	24				CHERRIES	2	15
BOIL	1	24	**C**			CHEW	2	15
BOOK	1	24	CABBAGE	1	27	CHICKEN (or HEN)	2	15
BORED (or DULL)	1	24	CAKE	1	27	CHINA	1	30
BORN	1	24	CAMEL	2	13	CHIPS	2	15
BORROW	1	25	CAMERA	1	28	CHOCOLATE	1	30
BOTH	1	25	CAN	1	28	CHOOSE	1	30
BOTH (Alternative)	2	12	CANADA	2	13	CHRISTIAN	2	16
BOY	1	25	CAN'T	1	28	CHRISTMAS	1	31
BRAVE (or POWER)	1	25	CAR	1	28	CHURCH	1	30
BREAK	1	25	CARAVAN	2	14	CINEMA	1	31